Carslaw's Sequences

Carslaw's Sequences

Poems by

Lisa M. Steinman

 UNIVERSITY OF TAMPA PRESS • TAMPA, FLORIDA • 2003

Manufactured in the United States of America
Book design by Richard Mathews
Printed on acid-free paper ∞
First Edition

University of Tampa Press
401 West Kennedy Blvd.
Tampa, FL 33606

ISBN 1-879852-86-1 (pbk)

Browse & order online at

http://utpress.ut.edu

Library of Congress Cataloging in Publication Data

Steinman, Lisa Malinowski, 1950-
  Carslaw's Sequences : poems / by Lisa M. Steinman.–1st ed.
    p. cm.
  ISBN 1-879852-86-1 (pbk. : alk. Paper)
I. Title
PS3569.T3793 C37 2003
  811'.54–dc21   2003002122

For Jim Shugrue

Contents

[2]

[3]

Foreword

I remember vividly the excitement I felt on first encountering Lisa Steinman and her poems, twelve years ago in Longview, Washington. I recognized at once that we were kindred spirits, sharing a passionate love of language and, consequently, of dictionaries. An interest in the diction and syntax of signs was another common bond.

Since then, we have managed to stay in touch as Lisa's poems chart new directions, explore unfamiliar territory. Her true subject is the life of the mind, to which she brings a keen sense of disparity and nuance. For her, "the world is verbose," "a waiting room for poems" that are more than worth the wait. Unlike Carslaw's sequences, Steinman's divergent series of "numbers" *do* add up. They are witty, serious, startling in their originality, and utterly unpredictable. This is a stunning book, one to return to again and again.

—Madeline DeFrees

Horatio Scott Carslaw: An early twentieth-century
mathematician who worked on divergent series, series
of numbers that cannot be summed, or that do not add up.

—*Dictionary of Science and Scientists*

Carslaw's Sequences

[1]

Carslaw's Sequences

This could be a poem about Carroll, the sweet
vacant boy from my school. His father had a dairy until
his brother fell from a milk truck's open seat,
delivered to eternity, making Carroll more fragile
and precious in his milky skin. One saw too the love
of fathers could be a dangerous thing.

Like Mirror Lake where I grew up skating under pines
and ghosts of southbound ducks. Or, above, the spire
of the church we climbed, lured by its converging lines
that got mixed with the trees and the skaters' campfire
in the ungiving lake, deaf to the warnings of fathers
who thought of milk trucks, dire consequences, and loss.

I've heard of a town that found a new name on television:
Truth or Consequences, New Mexico. The truth is they wish
to live forever. They want fame, a worthy modern mission.
The consequence is they are famous, but also maybe foolish,
as I am lying here next to my lover, a cat buttoned between
us. I'm wondering if the citizens of Pompeii composed

themselves, each night put their lives in order, for display.
The cat uncoils and rolls on his back — an Odalisque.
A mountain also rumbles at the edges of our city.
My mind drifts to cats and volcanoes, those grotesques
with which we live. All night, my dreams break on unkempt
shores where sand crabs flip like bits of debris. Or

[3]

I spend the night in a repair shop where nothing seems
to get fixed: no light bulbs, homes, forms in triplicate.
I'm afraid another world falls away during such dreams
of trivia, a world of burning bushes unrelated to domestic
chores or fire regulations. It's full of voices I can almost
taste. Which shows the difference between the seductions

of need and the consummations of sense—prosaic, hard won,
common as rock crystal. For instance, a young man surrounded
by loving aunts in the airport pretends to shoot down planes, for fun.
His body is twenty; his mind faltered somewhere and got grounded.
Aristotle says to live a good life a person must think. I think
the young man's life's not bad. We all live in a diminished world.

As planes bite the dust, the young man's cheers fill the empty
air. I try hard not to imagine disaster. I am fond
of my life, though more and more I hear a quiet *yes* when I
think of not living forever. From Minnesota, and blond,
the pilot arrives early. We all sprint for the exit together.
Back home, flocks of birds sit in the maple tree. The cat crouches

below. The birds chorus: *milk and honey, milk and honey.* The cat
replies: *milk trucks, laundry lists, truth <u>and</u> consequences.*

Life Stories: A Letter to an Acquaintance

> I will regard as good the exiles.
> —Jeremiah 24:5
> We are lined with eyes; we see with our feet.
> —Emerson

Welcome Home, Al, says the hand-painted banner stretched
over the garage door near the tidy corner house. I envy
Al these wobbling letters. Where has he been—the army?
summer camp? a prodigal, forgiven with this sign

for leaving? They sent out a telegram, and he
replied that very night that he'd be back in time for
cornflakes. Each night I dream, the alarm comes as a door
slamming. The world, which should be washed clean, is

washed out, by rain. The birds puff to twice their normal size
as if they could frighten rain away. Tonight, when
the phone interrupts me, I am dreaming again:
I want my life to have a shape, which I take to mean I want to die

having lived well. The notecard I'm handed says *wee, wee,*
which either means *yes yes* or tells me how small-minded I
am, or—involving my father, who is gone, counting my
toes, which still grip the earth—this will show me the way home.

Across the street, a woman with a husband who is dying
mourns the loss of her cat. Spring is in the air: oppressive
and dank. She vows she'll stop loving what's alive,
and recommends stuffed animals and God. *I* think

I should write to my mother who has always been too close
to need letters, but is now washing and ironing to save her
soul. But you are calling to tell me your jaw and teeth were
just broken by thugs on the sidewalks of our small town.

I can hear how frightened you are. It's catching. I am most afraid
that you've crawled back to rented rooms and now don't want to
intrude. *Excuse me,* you say, *I'm sorry to bother you.*
I hear: *Is this an emergency?* Outside, Al's sign sags in the rain.

I think of Jeremiah calling *O earth* to
what is absent, not palpable. But I get carried away.
We have no prophets and it's cold comfort—though I still say
we're too ruthless—that nothing can be called alien here.

Distant Friends

That year we both lost fathers, even though,
natural aristocrat, you didn't say so
while I spoke of nothing else. For me

the world was like a country road running
between field burns gone out of control, turning
the air acrid and opaque with smoke,

and what I mourned—lost comfort or stove-in
safety, haven, or, more simply, the loving—
I could not say then. Now, years later,

I wonder at you, seeming so able
outwardly, but underneath like a small bull
terrier wrestling with an intruder

or bone. It still seems a kind of wisdom
to me looking back: such delicate tact or calm,
practiced loss dexterously plowed under.

Shelley to Byron,
on Being Given an Already Named Boat

I'd wanted the name *Ariel*, so it could be
a music maker strumming the water, genie
of transformation, a conjugator of lamp
light's sudden rightnesses, and not this bad taste vamp
leading me on or fatuously giving rise
to desires that turn sour as I see the late skies
becoming all one color, though still receding.
With your name, the *Don Juan* plows the waves, needing
always to find something new, then finding the new
is just what's expected. I suppose that my crew
doesn't have the sense I have of what we will find.
Although my lover's husband, maybe, is resigned
to share my deathbed too. But what of the boy whose
name even I keep forgetting; he didn't choose
this battle between *Ariel* and *Don Juan*.

A battle I may lose. Though I've scorned the body—
the mind is not a matter of biology—
I push aside thoughts of the boy's loss as a pet
bird throws seed to the floor, profligate, but with regret.
We've confused the boy. He signed on with *Ariel*
thinking to caress the waves' rise and fall, each swell
left behind lightly, light flirting with surfaces.
The boy's talk is breezy; his laughter, nervous. His
nonchalance is not the form in which I wanted
loss of self either. What am I doing, haunted
by names foisted on me? I think of how the boat's
sail, badly erased with turpentine—creosote

would be more apt—preserves its standard. The mind's knack
for yielding to what's on canvas painted in black
letters defeats me. The boy says *I'm* Don Juan,

joking; he sees how wildly I try to outrun
the name I too, unwillingly, find on my tongue.
I used to love how, unsettled, desire lit
the world in unlooked-for ways. Unsettling as it
is, this argument lights nothing. I'm no roué—
but will not settle for second best. With dismay
I see all desire will force me to repeat
your lines. And yet to want nothing is to defeat
myself, or become subject to the malady
I can't bear: the tediousness of day-to-day
routine. The *Ariel* was supposed to outrace
tedium and leave self in its wake. We embrace
this wish so fondly, there's no one, when the storm comes,
who'll wing it, accept from the wind the many names
it traces and retraces on the bay's blank ruin.

A Poem of the Mind in Summer

I want the mind laid bare in motion,
like those instructional toys children
always call the invisible man or woman,
though officially they are visible.

Still, the kids aren't all wrong.
The man I carefully assembled
to get him right, organ by organ,
in his clear plastic skin.

He had overlays of sinew, muscle,
and soft tissue so hard its enamel
clicked on linoleum where I laid him
out as if on an assembly line.

I didn't like the woman as well,
always barefoot and pregnant,
less abstract than abstracted. I recall
their impossibly correct

posture over which I bent inhaling
paint fumes and glue, a model
citizen. Once they were put together,
I never dressed them; they never

asked each other out, just stood there,
hands clenched, chock full of livers,
entrails, lungs, and shelved like unread
books, spines unbroken. Just so,

populations of farms, houses, airplanes
were abandoned like factory towns,
no inner resources after all. The moral:
what's assembled is over

and done with. What failure
in the imagination of day-to-day,
the hyphens always more interesting
than the nouns they cement.

Stock Figures

Var vant kyr. –Old Norse
The poet must have more stomachs than a cow. –Thoreau

Bored and fleeing our neighbors
who think nature abhors
an hour without the sounds
of garden tools—though what

they find in these small suburban
yards to trim, edge, mow,
and prune at such length,
I can't imagine—we go out.

And find ourselves in bad company,
sitting at sidewalk tables
gazing at a storefront across the street:
"Bliss Machine Repairs Inc."

We are not finding it
so quiet after all, overhearing
the two men at the next table.
Did someone mention happiness?

What about generosity?
One young man explains, "I liked her.
We slept together, but
it was platonic." Biology, he

explains further, is destiny.
I chew on the question of how
he thinks the world might work.
Or play. And what of the anonymous

she in this story? What's
her description of the morning after
and the one after that? The story
is like a lumpy clay sculpture

made by a relative in grammar school,
something you can't admire
but must not throw away.
Wanting, I gather, is ungenerous.

Yet I want the two young men
to take themselves away
soon. Can one want desire,
I wonder, and—back home

finally—open the dictionary
to find the word, *wanting*,
involving deficiency
and lack, from the Old Norse

for which I am given a sentence:
"A cow was missing."
The cows are wanting. Related to
scant, thwart, wane, having nothing

to do with *wanton*, although suddenly,
by a leap of bad faith,
I see cows wanton in a meadow.
They carry meal in their mouths.

They eye the moon, think
hard, and unearth questions.
Meanwhile the young men too live
with bad days, days without

any sign of the ripe meadows
on which we'd let our neighbors
run their loud machines
until the cows come home.

Conversation Piece

Out the window: small round birds are
edging to branch tips, eating buds,

impersonating flowers and
death. The birds speak familiarly,

as if conversations were like
weather: exchange, the ding an sich,

an intimate vernacular,
common. Not the way we used to

watch Oz burst into black and white,
pure transportation, no special

effects, but transformed, converted
to humbug. And here's the rub: "to

be familiar with" is to make
sharp turns, still, as in *version, verse,*

vertigo. When in Rome, Romans
just lived together. As simple

as that. No backing or forthing.
Talk entered the picture late. Fish

could be conversant earlier—
all glad animal movement, no

vows, currency, talismans of
the possible. If you wanted

to change your life, you'd have to move.
Meanwhile, I hear the dead curse me,

especially those who've lost their
names: "Another lonely woman.

What else is new?" "A lonely man"
has a different ring to it, but

it's small change. All biography
reads: "Look. Here. 'Do no harm.' Too late."

Elsewhere, small birds bloom on the ends
of branches, which bow down. It's like

magic, except it's gravity.
Speech transforms the ordinary,

but into what? Such waste: passing
words back and forth. We found a new

town, and name it *Grief.* It has no
birds, no entrails to read. Just what

was and what is, transformed, like that
wren appearing   suddenly   now.

Suddenly

Render and *tender* were taken over in English
without change to avoid collision with *rend*
and *tend*.

       – *The Oxford Dictionary of English Etymology*

Watching the local what they call news—
neighborhood gatherings, lost exotics
like emus, children gone one way
or another astray—suddenly,

amidst the always familiar
nearly identical artist's
renderings of the wanted, there, strange
and tough, a good friend's good daughter.

Her face is like those of people
in rooms where voracious roving
cameras break down the doors and enter.
The cats hide in the wastebasket.

If one read the cats, they'd say "Keep
everything." Or, maybe, "It's all
a waste." You can always tell someone
has tried to plump the cushions, arrange

flowers; they've hung pictures, or placed
knickknacks just so. And this despite
the desperadoes in the closet.
Who is the home invader? ... Not

[17]

that I'd want, in a dark alley . . .
But suddenly there's also "and what
do we do now?" and then years of
"what do we do next?" The dropping

of some organ in the chest, as if
stepping off a cliff face and wanting
to try *that* step again. The artist's
rendering. Rendered up. From *to give back,*

hand over. Submit. Recite. Hold,
as in prison (see *apprehend*).
This is not something the mind holds,
skittering away, glancing off this

and that, saying no to the breaks,
as in "Them's the . . . ." As in hearts,
tendered, useless, held to accounts
on which one cannot licitly draw.

Interjections and Conjunctions at Sunset

Browsing the pages of an old grammar, I see
the sky performs miracles that involve warring
pink and gray dragons, the colors of Chinese tea-
pots. The tempest is on the page.

The sky's fierce and civilized at once, but unversed
in care. Like our cat, who cultivates birds, making
his familiar yard a grave, as if to rehearse
his death. The world is as seen, though

the body has *its* imperatives. And the sky.
And our neighbor, who feels no love for cats, leaving
notes that say what she's found when she's looked outside:
squirrels, the birds, and a raccoon—

all dead. The mind keeps what it can: land, deeds, the sheen
on a pigeon's neck, changing in changing light in
the eye of a beholder: miracles are seen.
As in the obituaries,

which today, careless, eulogize a dancer who
"continued work until her death, her most recent
choreography." That's it. That will have to do.
"Alas," says the small ship sinking

in the corner of the page. "Hush, Behold, O fie.
My sister! Ah, my brother." Does the sun setting
cause such wonder because there's a man in the street
with a sign that says "Love Jesus.

God hates sin"? The connective's unclear. I, for one,
can't tell if this is exhortation or threat or
a small often overlooked part of speech, say, some
exercise in the grammar of

sudden emotions of the mind, of pain, pleasure,
or surprise . . . of our desire to choreograph
that to which we're beholden. Voilà. We measure
our lives. "Oh dear," says the ship. "Look."

Signs of the Times

"Topless—plus." The sign on the strip near the Li Po Tavern
insists that more is less. In the school cafeteria, young men learn
to get ahead by playing "Street Fighter II." But there is still dirt
under their fingernails, and a cold wind in Anaconda, and that bright

wonder in Mill City, where someone in despair has built a folly of bone
and paint. Nearby, another man makes bad sketches for loose change
and throws place names at the tourists: Astoria, Scappoose. He is a man
who has mastered all regions. Elsewhere, on the high desert range

people who live in trailers gather at the Dairy Queen to gawk
at outlanders, as if strangers were signs of doom. I used to think I knew
at least the owls and the waterfalls, the glowing landscapes. I knew.
And have lost. We collect the mugs from which we once drank,

and head out for the city. The candles on the tables in the jazz
club reflect off pane glass, blossom in memoriam in the street.
I listened to this same guitar the night my father changed. These days
we do not simply die. We dwindle. Or we meet

the beginnings of our end. My mother's voice on the phone went sad
and tinny, saying things were not so good that day my dad
began to end. More *is* less. I too have signs of doom, lists of places,
and, outside, the world, to Scofield's conversations with the bass, is

mourning as I stare at what's not mine,
that stone-like stuff, from which I build a folly of my own.

Double Rainbow

At the airport, a voice says "If alarms are sounding
around you, we suggest you leave." I vow I will
attend to all that's crossed my path—voices, the dying
plant with one leaf curled like an aging hand. Something about ill

winds goes here. The plant nourishes the eyes; the ear,
alert to the woman who talks about brain scans.
It's like a waiting room for poems. In the bar
there's a dancer trying for an ill-paid road job, as Mick

stumbles in with the woman in pink heels and the lone
man in the shiny blue suit lists nieces, cousins
twice removed. He keeps his distances close to home,
hands gripping his pint and wanting a friendly ear.

Mick and Lady Pink have no eyes for him; the dancer says she
can't afford the job. The blue man talks and no
one listens to his need: an ear, an eye. Mick asks for money;
outside, the sky is doing unusual things with rainbows.

This is too neat. What of the women speaking
of teeth; the men, of carburetors? The youth who yells
he does not like yogurt, who plays the radio so that noise
fills the room? His father yelling back? Or the smell

of garlic outside on the path? The evening, cars, light—
unearthly as the rhyme of the dead plant's leaf and the blue
man's hand? There's something missing here—a sense
of how these lives work, or do not; how the radio

touches dancer and drunken couple, but not both in the same way.
The radio says "Buy something special for your Mom for Mother's Day
because your mother is special." The rainbow speaks of gold
to the blue, family man, who says "What you reap, you sow."

Ornamentals

Billboards are full of ideas about Easter.
You say holidays of this ilk suggest
the world can be left behind. I say *ilk*
means *of a place* or *in the blood*, the wrong word,

surely, for what's mongrel and in exile. Here,
our air's the gray of about-to-rain, silent
except for birds. Like a fairy godmother,
air & birds promise something. What do the rocks

have to say to this? Sufficient unto.
Old as . . . no, older. I'd like the world
to sing and yield ideas and, yielding,
to keep on singing even in the gray air.

Weeks of rain say "Yeah, right," and erase the world.
Pleased to read that feathers devolved into
flight, you still make poems of things. I'm out
night fishing, rain fishing, watching the birds

return. There's music threatening in the wings.
A sign by the road says "Dinks. Thanks." Granted
three wishes, I'd want poems, a good death
for us, but none for the world. The spring rains

seem to require a song. I hear rain
in the hydrangea, the name of which escapes
and returns to blossom, seasonal,
perishable as fruit . . . things of this ilk.

Landscape with Boat

On vacation, and I'm already packing to go home
three days before departure, which is not so hot
with only two weeks away. Out the window,
on the horizon, if you squint, the shipping lane
winks back: ferry   barge   ferry.

Like one of the pens sold locally but made
in Denmark where the Lake District, Chicago,
and the San Juans are indistinguishable at one point
in the assembly. When you tip the pen to write,
a ship glides across the bay,

keeping the wheels of industry turning, at least
in Denmark where I imagine all differences
are crossed, all channels kept open. I have just
finished reading about how bad proletarian novels
were on gender and character:

fat was bad; women could be bitchy. And then
I read a poet, an old acquaintance, who returns,
like a dog worrying a bone, to his high school loves
or lovers, as if they will resurrect his body or his
hair. And behind all this sheer desire—

bodies fat or female, new-minted or old hat—
the boats cross and recross the channel
as if following some dotted line. The way I keep
thinking my life is more party line than the thriller
I'd once imagined.

She was born. She was promising. She grew up
and was as good as her word. The boats
keep channeling goods across the harbor, as I stand
here with my baggage, ready to ship out. No,
ship-shape, as usual.

[2]

Old Woman Poem

All summer the crows yelled at me from trees
in praise of the immaterial. Surly
I was by fall. The laundromat sign read:

"Re-grand opening." And the world did open,
garden notebooks filling with weeds—
meadow rue, lady's mantle, the first page

left blank for Elijah. Just in case. Though
the papers lamented the weapons of mass
destruction, as if destruction did not

occur to us one by one. Now passing
cars sing in warm rain, but not well, what with
their tin ears, petulant and off-kilter.

I wake up with a furrowed heart. I am
as cultivated as the delicate
smell of carrots thinned early. I can taste

my childhood. Look: a small figure dances
in the yard. No, look: it's me. No, I'm here
rehearsing the dance in memory, trying

to imagine an older woman's life.
Somehow I've come to feel such an untoward
affection for my younger self, I could

just cry. Instead, I thin carrots, hearing
crows, living carefully ... as if I might
otherwise forget to wake, eat, breathe.

Testimonials from the Boarding House

I

Next time, the fire. This time beset
by a drought so serious it's rearranged the land.
Where the stream used to be, there's a pit
mine with a causeway overlooking wrinkles of clay.

In her dream, Emily is looking for her cat,
all collared and white with tags that say
"The Sole Comfort of One Who Lives Alone"
or "Alcoa Aluminum." The search party is having trouble

because all things here have more than one name,
the one to which they do not answer and the one the state
requires. I know the search and drought are important. I think:
dry night of the soul. I think: she seeks what does not seek

her. I think: She will hazard Alcoa and dizzying heights
for a cat in a drought, while others with more sense
would look for shade or solid ground or go home,
that place from which I am always setting out.

II

Not quite like Broderick, who says he is standing in his cut-offs
watering his lawn, when the police sweep him up and ship him
to Detroit, on a warrant for someone named Roderick, who is tall
and heavy. Skinny and five-five, Broderick, released, hits
the streets of Detroit, weeks later, in his cut-offs. This is his tale.

III

At ninety-eight, my grandmother enters heaven.
When she meets my grandfather again, she will
wear pink, as always. But even if we disallow
the child in the boarding house with the verandah

and shelves full of seashore souvenirs;
the bride of unformed dreams, who married
the boarder—a student out of light opera,
washing windows for enlightenment—it's unclear

which woman he will meet. Even if we hold him
constant, sitting at some cloudy, heavenly
desk, translating Rilke for the last ten years, will she
step forward as the woman bitter over losing their home

and one child too many? Or the small resigned elder, all
dentures and Spic and Span? Or even older, the spruced-up
sharp-tongued mourner, who lost the man she grew used to
and then lost the memory of that loss, telling everyone

her husband was off on a trip? Will she recall not recalling?
Or will there be some awful celestial gaffe?

IV

Weldon Anderson and Trish and Dave seem to be looking
for the meaning of their lives. Says Weldon, his
mother was the first woman to own a trucking
company. He asks your name. He was the fastest
typist in Walla Walla, in 1940, and the record
has never been broken. He wants this on record.
Dave, says Trish's husband, over pasta at the café,
should be on record as a homewrecker. Loudly,
he says this over and over, until the police come.
Someone must put this all on record.

V

At first only the roof and then the windows ripple
with heat. A man lumbers out onto the porch as if he
had stumbled over the doorsill. The porch swing is
lined with figures whose limbs have been singed.

Someone is screaming orders: "Man the hoses." "Move
away." "Start the car." And then just the effect
of screaming or order or voice. What have we done?
Where there is smoke, there is ash, from which,
on the once green earth, no one rises.

Road Work

Slowed in traffic, I see hills differ from place to place:
each mountain with its own discrete name and hairpin turns, trailers,
wood smoke, although the road signs said there would be "no areas
for the next hundred miles." And these hills *are* so unfamiliar
my eyes don't know where to look. Outside the car window, a cat

conjures from movement its bird. One mile back, an eccentric,
homemade sign said "Caution. Flager," heralding the woman who
is leaning her head on her sign—*Slow*—in thought or exhaustion.
Then her sign says *Stop*. So we do. We do not need the man who—
overheard at lunch—said he taught leadership to prisoners

on death row. We don't know when we'll move on. We're like the week's
personality test, blanks waiting to be filled: "Anything
you can do _____: a) you ought to; b) would be appreciated;
c) I can do better." Meanwhile, the crosswalk here feels obliged
to say "Stop when occupied." And here I am *pre*occupied,

hoarding birds in flight, local color, public languages
in a place that looks like Egypt but promises no exile,
which would imply return. This roadside for someone else might hold
horsy colloquies, contentments of cows, homecoming parades.
Although at the Promised Land Truck Stop, a family huddles

near their dirt bikes as one man—son, husband—harangues his kin
about sloth; he's screaming his direction-less, dirt-bike-riding,
it's-all-wrong, hard-working anger. I am appalled that I think
I understand how he feels. Knowing just dampens my spirits,
as does the rain that's coming on. In the meantime, his family

is too under the considerable weather even
to look embarrassed. Nearby, a shop advertises "Bullets.
Three for one dollar." A sign, but of what? I've gotten as far
as bad for birds. Then the flagger waves, and I drive on under
gray skies so textured and vibrant, gray surely counts as color.

The Resurrection of Sight on Holiday

Sheep cascade down the mountains, with their two *e*'s
as in *genteel* or *veneer* or *seer*. Some lesser birds
of paradise display on a common tree;
they seem to await final things like a mind cluttered
with scraps of dismality. Against gray sky

a red balloon bobs up and down on a slate
roof, gains a head and body, and becomes a roofer
with a red cap. If you insist on brute fact
you end with global brutishness. There is a failure
of sight here, but the failure speaks. As we walk

the street, I'm keeping track of what mustn't fall
away: passport, return ticket, keys, wallet, and last
is myself. Unlike the sheep, we come when called.
Come the resurrection, we'll help other passengers,
as on a bus that's hit a bad bump and stalled;

we'll sit kicking our headstones. The bug I've killed
has left a dark spot on my coat: it rises with me,
judged not. It's a mosquito-eat-woman world,
after all. As the old woman on the bus says, trees
take the goodness from the soil. And the weathered

man with walking stick and old boots tells his friends
about wading into the lake to cut loose a duck
snarled in fishing line; careless, the man's toe sends
a stone flying, breaks his foot. Last time he'll do a duck
a good turn. Quite right, says one friend. God leans

down when he sees such deeds and thinks "I'll have *you*."
Walking the high road, we go past a dead sheep, its throat
thrown back, its skin soft as an old potato
and bristling with eyes. For a moment, it seems to gloat,
to be rolling in the grass for joy. Just so,

this new world should either cure the hum of days
in which we can't see sorrow stretched out like vistas
from a high place or figure in the landscape
what will stay and what is lost. The day's full of bird calls
and sheep and steep paths smelling of wild garlic.

Potatoes, Cabbages, Leeks, Plague, War

−a meditation on a line from Pascal about wretchedness

What *was* the man thinking? Why cabbages
and leeks? Like potatoes, rock solid.
You'd think a mathematician would play
by the numbers: simple, compound, or

imaginary. A child by the civic
monument yells "Hey, wait. Look. Art," then
hops between the pavement squares, singing
"Step on a crack. Break ... "

Divining danger in the concrete, he walks
on slight fractures, but counts on the familiar,
practicing a tactful forensics. His mother
diagnoses herself with obsessive-

compulsive disorder and incipient
Alzheimer's. A sad state when you cannot
recall what you're compelled to repeat.
Cabbages, leeks, potatoes. Compounded

of dirt and sun, tough green sprouts shrug off
the soil. Then plants, flowers, hung improbably
with small, green, lantern-like globes. Between
the rows, in the path, a small stone appears:

no, a potato, no, two, three, five,
eight, no: bouquets of potatoes,

hand gathered by forays—brief as
the body's delicate hold—on earth.

Are potatoes part of hunger then?
Hunger, sharp as blue cheese on bread with wine
fiery red as the sun on the south coast
from which it comes. The coast smells of fish and brine

in the town where an ordinary young man
pumps gas. He leans in windows, ominous
and amiable, giving change and judging
women's legs. He'll go fishing tomorrow.

If he were asked he'd say he loves his job,
which changes day to day, talk and money
passing back and forth. There's no reason to think
satisfaction is less complicated than desire.

Here, look: there's two more people on the town
sidewalk. His once-blond gray hair is
slicked back; he struts a little. His name
would be something like Dutch. He calls her "Mother."

After the army, he found a job fixing
small appliances. Heavy-set, she's just had
her hair done. You can tell she is pleased
with her new, bright green synthetic stretch pants.

They are holding hands absent-mindedly,
long-time companions. They are not thinking
about their complex compact of hands,
solid as solace, meat and potatoes.

No plague. No war. And not so simple:
meat and potatoes, cabbages, leeks. Mothers
and children, all falling through the cracks
of light where you'd least expect it.

Table Talk

Fricatives, plosives, glide to nose: the mainstays of food and wine
rolled round on the palate. Not the taste; the phrase, "of food and wine."

So I say. You say otherwise, arguing it is enough
to sing loudly, drink often, eat, and voice the praise of food and wine.

Call and response. Thirst and hunger call hunger and thirst. We take
turns, voice and body woven in medleys of food and wine.

Sauterne and cold crab, light pink and white, with mustard mayonnaise:
palette and palate joined in a bouillabaisse of food and wine.

I dream of a life full of soulful, timely language. You say:
"Forget milk and honey, roses; these are the days of *food* and wine."

That night I dreamt I knew the body's pleasures, and rose chanting
full-bodied Chianti, beef stew, warm bread—lays of food and wine.

You know the physical world includes the tongue. Our *ohs* and *ayes*
clearly nourish those who are wise in the ways of food and wine.

Small Fall Song

Something is about to leave and we
can't legislate its love. The world, its look,
fat & physical, feeding the eye,
the tongue & skin, that fleshy nook
behind the knee. It's not bark, oak tree,

an entry in some index. It's autumn. It's dying.
But not without a long, slow, sweet, sweet...
The leaves redden like fruit. The air, clean as ...
In the canyon, heron dally with the air in

flight. *Yes*, we say to the world at times. And *yes. Come.*

[3]

Millennial Ode

The hand's pleasure writing all those O's,
sweet nothings, like the sweet voicing

of the roman numerals, MM. Not beginning,
middle, end. Just   day   day   day

stretched out like a field in Ohio. Dark birds
plummet past the window, preying

on other birds. The season should be dark
glints of light off frozen branches, snow,

but you're out barefoot looking under vines,
cars, trees, for the daily news that does not

arrive: the paper boy's sleight of hand.
See here? A child weeps over a lost tree branch

his older brother has added to the fire.
But look what a beautiful flame it's made,

says his mother. She gestures toward heat
without heft. The branch fit right

in his hand, not to mention its virtue
as a weapon against older brothers.

You'll have it in memory, says his father,
thinking, no, you'll have memories of this

betrayal of the physical, a score to settle,
boy and world tied—OO—for years to come.

The Object of Cross-Country Driving

*—on seeing an exhibit of work by Gail and
Zachariah Rieke in the Santa Fe Museum
of Fine Arts*

"Found objects continue to have their own
histories. Meanings multiply and shift
constantly while the constituent parts

retain particularity, showing the artists' desire
to be supple about context and association," says
the catalogue. It goes on about how objects are released

to be themselves, here in the museum
in Santa Fe. Suddenly, transported,
I think of Brisco Stubblefield, who aids

travelers at rest stops unsolicited, red suspenders
over his sixty-something-year-old belly. His capacity
for indecision is monumental. After he retired,

he says, he ran for office, went into antiques, into junk,
including used refrigerators, into glassware, into
teaching, a PhD program, into maligning all those

different than he is. Although what or who he is
is not clear. He does make clear he does not like change.
He's like a chameleon's habitat, he makes us—

me and my husband—grow silent, faced with his talk of "them"
and "things going downhill," of urban crime, of skin color.
An unattractive shape shifter, he's trying to place us

[49]

though his sense of geography leaves something
to be desired. Noticing our license plates
are falling off, he offers help: wire and pliers

and talk, in which he rearranges all the maps, transplanting
the Pacific Northwest to somewhere near the Colorado
Plateau. He gives us red cedars in Zion National Park's

layers of limestone, mudstones, shale, sandstone
uplifting, trading places with the pinyon,
brush, and hoodoos. Brisco, then, is generous

and all imagination, while we drive
through his state seeing only square and round
bales; we keep ourselves awake trading words

that begin with v until we have exhausted our store.
I'd thought geography was secure, rock-solid, moving
only in geology's sweet time. Yet for a second

I'm translated by Brisco, almost as I am by what is
in this show in Santa Fe. Translated, but not transplanted.
"I like to cause trouble," Brisco says, and he does. When we leave

him, reattached to plates put back in place,
the shadows of phone wires above trace thin
connecting lines on the Ohio roads,

of which we take him to be an atypical denizen.
I had wanted him to have his own poem, his own unique say,
but I've come to think it can't be done. He's become something else,

like the Kronos Quartet on the radio
in Kansas playing Hendrix, or the sea shells
from the Atlantic on our dashboard growing

more souvenir-like and exotic as we head home.
Brisco is by now some installation I could call
"Buckeye, Confused or Confusing," "Frightening Person:

Ohio," or "Solid Citizen." Geography may be
places and the people who talk and live in them. But then who
is this man who's moved into my museum in Santa Fe,

where I can tell he doesn't particularly
like the exhibit. Our tastes differ. He's really
not taken with the art, although he has the grace

to be embarrassed by this. As for me,
I can't seem to let him go, this buck-eyed
collector of doodads, mythographer,

gerrymanderer of people, even those whose license
plates are not the right color. We all hold our ground,
no one giving an inch, each unwilling to be moved.

Toyota Celica Sestina

Four women who have brought their cars in for repair
sit on the hard plastic seats of the waiting room,
eight eyes full front, turned to the television set
that tells them they need to find a hobby—to read
or paint, to be creative. Meanwhile, the car shop's
loudspeaker flickers on and off, joining the act

as salesmen page customers. There is a one-act
play in town, the TV talk show says, that re-pairs
Stiller and Meara. Theater's better for you than shop-
ping or less active pastimes. You want culture. Room
to grow. Books. Although it's impossible to read
here, with the broadcast noises and the people set-

tled in orange plastic, as if they have been set
here for life. An older woman, aqua-clad, acts
distraught, the price beyond her means, as she is read
a litany of parts, brakes, labor, the repairs
she needs. The others keep still in the waiting room
as if she's on TV, and the service rep's shop-

talk's for their benefit, too, along with the shop-
worn chairs and linoleum and TV upset
with them for not reading, although the ladies room
is the only quiet place around, and it acts
as a refuge for the saleswomen, who repair
there to discuss makeup, clothes, and jobs, not ready

for the customers in the outdoor lot who read
sticker prices and mention trade-ins as they shop
for new cars. The TV says its show will re-air
Tuesday; it warns again of the dangers of sit-
ting still, telling everyone to clean up their acts
and renew their creative spirits. There's no room

here to love what you do. Back in the waiting room,
in their laps, the women all *have* something to read,
though their books have slid from their hands as they react
to the TV, public address, small-time car shop
dramas. The cashier tells one woman she's all set
to go; her car at least is now in good repair,

no longer acting up. She leaves the auto shop
waiting room after gathering her things and settling
her bill, trying to read the outside, winter air.

Anticipating House Guests

I

After a week cleaning house, my hands are numb. So Saturday
we set out to hike around a lake, and the ranger says "No,
there's all kinds of snow in Indian Heaven." Just like the sign
on Mt. Rainier says "The road to Paradise is always open."

Although of course it's not. The ranger has rained on our parade
and we go home in cool, green light. I think a thing of beauty's
a joy forever, but what is this clean kitchen to which we
give a week? Even in memory, it will be less joy than pain,

though it has its moments. One friend says "Ah, a V-8 moment."
Another says cleaning is like sorbet; it clears the palate.
It seems clear, one way or another. "Look, Ma," I say. "No hands."
Meanwhile, my parents sit upright in the parlor, silhouettes

in whose dark outlines I move. There is no paradise although
I try to make one for my guests. For each meal my grandmother
                                                    would change
the butter dish. My mother doesn't. I could have walked
to Paradise. Practice makes perfect the life we imagine.

II

Two women, young, cruise the streets, eager to get to the party.
They know this street. It's full of life and they are too, out for fun,
irked at the old couple going too slowly in front of them,
who won't be rushed by horns. So the young woman at the wheel guns

the engine, swings out to pass, turns back to glare. She doesn't see
they've slowed for people at the crosswalk; she's surprised when she hits
the first one, when a body flies overhead. When the second
one down gets up, first it's like a cartoon. Everyone swears, sits
up, and carries on to the next reel. But what is has changed:
for the body, for the couple. Finally, the young woman might
reimagine the world — they came out of nowhere, their own fault.
And it's Friday night with crowds and flashing emergency lights . . .

III

It's a police story. It's okay. In my story, I clean
pots, handles, hooks, the wall on which they hang. I see how endless
practice is. I have no butter dish, but I do imagine
my kitchen—not the cleaning of it, but some kind of heaven

for house guests, where numb hands do not exist. You know how it goes.
In a novel, the body would struggle back to life. Or not.
The young driver would become a villain or a nun. The old
couple tells the story a few times and then goes on with life.

They make it new. Here, we don't know how it ends because, except
perhaps for the airborne body, whose life I can't imagine,
it does not end. Gloom stomps around the house saying "Don't mind me,"
while under its breath muttering a somewhat different story.

Marriage–

a state or action that's been called a form
of friendship recognized by the police,
blending tradition and modernity,

like the mix in the name of a local
store, "The Vinyl Bridal Shoppe." Or in the
names given by a neighborhood woman

to her three kids: Mannix, Starsky and Hutch,
and George. A singular institution
made of dreams and discussions of who'll do

dishes. Of learning it's small potatoes
if, while clearing the table, one of you
always leaves behind a solitary

fork or spoon "to appease the gods," or that
only one of you believes doors can be
left open ... that one of you collects

kewpie dolls, while the other's passionate
about divestment. You need not expect
that you'll share absolutely everything:

old friends and tee shirts and taste. So you make
do, make it up as you go along, wing
it to discover, near the unwashed socks,

piles of discarded words: *uxorious,*
husbandry, covenant, to bind, wedlock,
having or *taking,* although you can still

hold affection. Whatever marriage is,
it no longer appears to be simple.
It's certainly not "he said, she said," though

it may be "I said, we said." Of course, this
is a dialogue. "Hello," she says to
the winter sun each morning. "Hello, your-

self," he says back. It's an estate of peace—
"of liberty and union," as Webster's
statue says. Nuptials, like fields

of potatoes or grain, give sustenance.
As when, up late arguing, no one yields,
but each rises next morning converted.

Or when the leaver of cutlery clears
everything away, and, disconcerted,
the other misses stray forks on the table

after meals. The married speak in the first
person plural, the unfashionable
'we' without which there's no 'I' to speak of,

no 'you' to speak to, no people in places
held in common. At root, marriage hovers
between "good luck" and "congratulations,"

between the done and the beginning. We
still tie knots & say "I do," one on one
daily, in the first person, in the flesh,

which is why we still throw rice at weddings—
to show it's not against the grain, this two-
sided consensual negotiation.

Night Work

Tonight, I'm standing in a landscape where
the wind tosses the trees; the sky mumbles
constantly; visions unfold; waterfalls—

domestic and wild at once—say hard things
brilliantly. The world is verbose, flickers
of thought around every corner that hint

of another landscape where nothing speaks.
I read about diamond cutters. Diamonds
in the rough are metaphors for what comes

when we call *beauty.* Or *light.* Or *money.*
How can you tell what's real? Yet do you doubt
we're really here? That here is one hand; here,

another? The sky does have a glitter,
light promising snow, again. Poems walk by:
He said. She said. But it's too cold to tell

the whole story. The seed catalogues give
no assurance of gardens. They offer
contests. I pick the green convertible, but

the voice of desire has no hand in this.
The diamond cutters make off with their jewels.
I think, *Damn it. Who says they will come back?*

I do see the world is saying nothing
quite clearly. It is cold. And I can hear
the sound that wind makes when there are no leaves.

Snow and *Praise*

The radio touts two girls who sing as three.
I wonder if one sings as two. Or is each one
in voice and a half? I read, meanwhile, on TV
(printed under mothers with candy canes)
"This is your personal invitation. Come

to our sale." These thoughts, as soon as they're raised,
get lost in the small demands of household chores.
As I work, I belt out songs that start with *Snow* and *Praise*.
What's left outside our songs is left at loose
ends. I wrestle with the season, for

I would be blessed. Icicles halo the back
porch. I chop garlic, mushrooms, bok choy.
The cat races around the house, a maniac,
then settles in. The way some words—*faithful*
or *breadfruit*—open a place in the heart for joy

and then find something else in residence
there. *Breadfruit*: what vegetable could live up
to such a glowing name? Speaking of sustenance,
Edenic, filling? Children sing outside
the door, caroling, oblivious

to cold; one voice insists they've not sung all
of *All Ye Faithful*. Songs stop and other voices
agree with her, though as many faithful
as there are have come. I chop and listen to this
ragged choir, preferring it to the choices

on TV. I like these eight who think as twelve.
And I recall how, buying vegetables,
I met a man from work who said, leaning on shelves
full of squash, that we must talk of poems . . .
but not near broccoli in a neat hedge, tables

of mushrooms. He worries about rhyming verse
with produce. Back home with this conversation
in mind, I sit at my desk, dinner on the verge
of ruin. The cat leaps up sending flurries
of paper to the floor, insisting on attention

he does not really want, his hind leg thrust
above his head, head bent to tail. This
makes me look up. Camellias in the snow burst
into bloom, like children into song. It seems
they must have sung outside my awareness

of them for days, mixed with the cat's pose,
the broccoli, the weather, the Christmas snowfall.
I take them to heart, just as if they're things I chose.
The radio plays in the background. Suddenly
I feel like one girl who can't sing at all.

Canyon. Ode.

> I used to think poetry would change the
> world, back when I was all imagination.
>
> —Wallace Stevens

The rose appears   daily
on the walk between work and home.   Every wire
in this suburb has its bird,   burnished

                                        & sullen.
   What the birds should discuss is
       the feeling to which landscapes answer.   And the ground:
       the place names that *are* the ground. Against the red maple and mist
a yellow sign says "No outlet"

          —as if normally we could plug directly into the numinous fall
       behind the scalloped picket fence,   the pumpkin set out
for All Souls', the pine needles draped over laurel,
       the round, brownish stubs of anemone,   the moment between
yes and *no*, walking from home
to work.

          The rose sets itself against gray sky
               and mouths platitudes.
The world says "I *could* have made you

                              a mushroom or an onion."

Here there's dusty miller and a plastic pumpkin-bag
                          filled with fallen leaves, waste, sunlight.
    "No outlet."

Behind the houses, a canyon yaws   an emphasis   a conduit.
It goes without saying
                          I can hear voices
                                —many women, a few men, some crippled
                          by age or disease or grief some who cannot admit
        food or air   barely
                          audible, people I cannot say
        I love

Standing on the edge of this gradual decline
called a canyon   a sag   hearing
              a response   echoes, which measure the shape and depth
        of emptiness

        I am of two minds
                          like a tree with two birds.
        The common crow. Delights in carrion.
        Corvus corvus, the name
        of echoes.

        Another bird for which the book

of common birds   of the region
has no name.

Sound bounces off the tidy yards and houses   with their family
resemblances.
                If I jumped from here
                I would not take flight.

The echoes sometimes flood the neighborhood
skimmia,   curls of frost,   "Dead End"   and
                a license plate that says "Yo"
                        asserting itself, calling, and embarrassed
about it.   The circular mouth of a birdhouse   silent.
Which is just as well.   If it launched into

                                        speech
                        it would say   something—
under its breath—   about birds and hands and bushes.

The neighborhood watch has set out a concrete garbage can.   In it, I see
a poster, waste, with a wren   black and white and blue   that says
"Sale. Today."

                This could be frightening. Suddenly
                the laurel is muttering. The andromeda
                whining about someone its small leaves

flapping to attract attention.
                              Small talk is not
what I want   from shrubs   but what can you expect?

This space walking between
                              could be a world of its own.

Acknowledgments

The following poems, some in earlier versions, first appeared in the following journals, and are reprinted here with thanks to the editors: "Marriage" in *Epoch*; "Small Fall Song" and "Anticipating House Guests" in *The Women's Review of Books*; "Canyon. Ode." in *So To Speak*; "Potatoes, Cabbages, Leeks, Plague, War," "Road Work," and "The Object of Cross-Country Driving" in *Notre Dame Review*; "Suddenly" and "Table Talk" in *Prairie Schooner*; "Carslaw's Sequences" in *Poetry East*; "Signs of the Times" in *New Virginia Quarterly*; "Testimonials from the Boarding House" in *Michigan Quarterly*; "Shelley to Byron, On Being Given An Already Named Boat" in *Threepenny Review*; "Double Rainbow" and "Toyota Celica Sestina" in *Quarterly West*; "Landscape With Boat," "A Poem of the Mind in Summer" and "Life Stories: A Letter to an Acquaintance" in *Birmingham Poetry Review*; "The Resurrection of Sight on Holiday" in *International Quarterly*; "Old Woman Poem" in *Born Magazine*; and "Ornamentals" in *The Chariton Review*.

About the Artist

Gail Rieke is a collage/assemblage artist who received her BFA and MFA from the University of Florida. She has travelled and taught in the U.S. and Canada and is represented in permanent collections including the Museum of New Mexico, Albuquerque Museum, Sheldon Memorial Art Gallery of the University of Nebraska, Roswell Museum, The Santa Fe Institute, and many private collections. She has been featured in *Fiberarts* and *Artspace* magazines and in the recent books, *Contemporary Art in New Mexico* and *Creative Collaboration*. Gail shares a home/studio/gallery in Santa Fe with her husband and frequent collaborator, painter Zachariah Rieke. Their 2000 retrospective at the Museum of Fine Arts in Santa Fe, *Gail & Zachariah Rieke: Found Objects in an Open World*, remains influential through a printed catalog by the same name. They have three children.

About the Author

Lisa M. Steinman was born and raised in rural Connecticut, daughter of a mathematician, which she suspects is one reason why the title and concept for *Carslaw's Sequences* appealed to her. She attended college and graduate school at Cornell University in rural upstate New York where she worked with A. R. Ammons and William Matthews, completing both MFA and PhD degrees. Her poetry frequently appears in journals, periodicals, and anthologies, and her books and chapbooks include *Lost Poems* (Ithaca House, 1976), *All That Comes to Light* (Arrowood Books, 1989), *A Book of Other Days* (Arrowood Books, 1993), and *Ordinary Songs* (26 Books, 1996). For the past twenty-seven years she has taught at Reed College, writing and living in Portland, Oregon, with her husband, Jim Shugrue, also a writer. Together they have edited the poetry magazine *Hubbub* for the past twenty years.

About the Book

Carslaw's Sequences is set in Aurelia types designed by Hermann Zapf in 1983 and released for digital composition by the Elsner & Flake Foundry of Hamburg, Germany. Mr. Zapf suggests both a distinguished ancestry and a modern identity for his Aurelia font: "A design in the style of the roman used by Nicolas Jenson in Venice after 1470, but it is shaped for the digital photocomposing equipment of today. The type is named after the Roman emperor Aurelianus, who built the Via Aurelia in Italy." The book was printed on acid-free Glatfelter Supple Opaque Natural recycled text papers, and it was designed and typeset by Richard Mathews at the University of Tampa Press.

POETRY FROM THE UNIVERSITY OF TAMPA PRESS

Jenny Browne, *At Once*

Richard Chess, *Tekiah*

Richard Chess, *Chair in the Desert*

Kathleen Jesme, *Fire Eater*

John Willis Menard, *Lays in Summer Lands*

Jordan Smith, *For Appearances* (WINNER OF THE TAMPA REVIEW PRIZE FOR POETRY)

Lisa M. Steinman, *Carslaw's Sequences*

Richard Terrill, *Coming Late to Rachmaninoff*